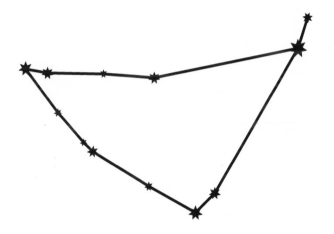

ONE IDEA PRESS

For permission requests, write to the publisher, addressed
"Attention: Permissions Request," at the following email address:
hello@oneideapress.com

Ordering Information:
Quantity sales. Special discounts are available on quantity purchases by
corporations, associations, and others. For details, contact the "Special Sales
Department" at the following email address: hello@oneideapress.com.

Paperback Edition: 978-1-944134-69-3
Hardback Edition: 978-1-944134-80-8

Printed in the United States of America

Capricorn

a love letter

Heidi Rose Robbins

with illustrations by
Wyoh Lee

hello love.

(yes, you)

Friends,

I'm so glad you are holding this book! It is filled with encouragement and an ongoing invitation for us all to be more fully who we are.

The best way to work with these books is to purchase one for each of your signs — your Sun, Moon, and Rising Sign.

These are the three most important positions in your astrological chart. You can discover what these are if you enter your exact time, date, and place of birth in any online astrology site. Each position has something unique to offer.

When you read the book for your Moon, think of it as an energy that is very available to you. It's a place where you might feel comfortable. The Moon has to do with our emotional life, our patterns of behavior, and circumstances of our childhood. We can rely on the Moon, but we also want to work to shed the patterns that no longer serve us.

The Sun is our present personality. We can learn a lot about our everyday self in the world. We can learn about the energies we have readily available to us to use in service to our highest calling.

The Rising Sign is the most important point. It is the sign that was rising as we took our first breath. It holds the key to our soul's calling. It is an energy we want to cultivate and be generous with throughout our lives.

So — enjoy the journey. Be sure to read them all!

Welcome
{13}

11

My dear Capricorn,

This little book is a love letter to your wise and hard working self. It is written to remind you of your many gifts. It is written to be a loving mirror so any page can remind you who you truly are. Take it in, dear Capricorn. Breathe in the rigor and responsibility that is YOU. See your deliberate, powerful self in these pages.

This little book will also explore those places in ourselves that start to close when we want to open, the part of us that hesitates when we want to act. We all have our quirks and difficulties, after all. But if we return again and again to our potency, vulnerability, and sense of possibility, we can outgrow our closures one by one.

Think of this book as a treasure chest containing the golden coins of YOU. Open it when you wish to remember your beauty, worth or great potential. And remember, too, this Capricorn part of you is just one voice in the symphony of YOU. It cannot possibly contain your complexity and bounty. But it can begin to name just a few of your gifts.

Read this out loud when you can. Read this in the morning. Read it before bed. Read it when you need encouragement. Read it even if you are already feeling full of commitment and determination. Let it fuel you. Own it and use it and claim it! This is your love letter, Capricorn. This is the song of YOU.

Big love,
Heidi Rose

Celebrating Capricorn

As you read this celebration, you will sometimes say "Yes, yes, yes! This is me!" And you may likewise sometimes feel that you have not yet lived into some of these qualities. This is honoring and celebrating the very best of your Capricorn energy. This is naming the full, conscious, awakened use of your Capricorn gifts. We are sounding the note of THE POSSIBLE. So, even if you feel you still have work to do in certain areas — as do we all — let these words be inspiration to offer your best Self!

♑

You embody purpose
and commitment.

You know how to take charge of
your life, Capricorn. You are a
natural leader. The moment you
walk into a room, it is clear you
are committed. You are in charge
of your life.

♑

You are cool and clear,
wise and collected.

You are not easily ruffled, dear
Capricorn. You are steady and
grounded. You don't lose your
composure often. You make the
next, most sensible, clear choice.

♑

You achieve what you set
out to achieve.

You climb the mountain. You set
your sights and begin. Often from
a very young age, you know where
you are headed and you don't
give up until you get there.

♑

You are determined.

You possess a certain grit. You dig in when others might quit. You see it through. You push when you need to push. If it can be done, you will do it. Purpose is your middle name.

♑

You are sure-footed.

Have you ever seen a mountain
goat actually climb a mountain,
dear Capricorn? It's a sight
to behold. They can balance
and grip in the most precarious
situations. You are like that too.
You stay on course.

You are intuitive.

Remember, Capricorn is half goat, half fish. You know something about the heights and something about the depths. Your connection to the timelessness of the earth actually feeds your intuitive connection with the natural world and its rhythms.

You always do what you say
you're going to do.

There isn't a lot of time to PLAY in
your world, dear Capricorn. There
is work to be done and you do
it. You don't abandon what you
have given yourself to do. You see
it through. You commit.

♑

You have a good sense of humor.

Yes, thank goodness! You are funny. You take life so seriously that you need a release valve. Your motto might be something like, "Life is very serious. Take it lightly." This is one of your saving graces!

♑

You assume responsibility with ease.

You are the parent in the room. People turn to you for help. You respond to what is needed. You have an innate drive to protect others and do the right thing. You follow the rules.

♑

You are a great director.

You know how to manage people and time! You know how to give structure to chaos. This makes you a great director, manager or CEO. You don't mind being in charge and you excel when you are given big responsibility.

♑

You execute the plan well.

You want to know the plan and all its particulars. You want to understand the plan from every angle. You want to know what is expected. Once all that is in place, you are masterful at seeing any plan through. You lead the way.

♑

You climb.

The summit is where you want to be. You want to be the best at what you do. Why be less? You don't rush or skip steps. You steadily climb. And yes, you reach the summit when the time is exactly right.

You do the work.

The fact is, the people who succeed, as you wish to succeed, also understand there is work to be done. You don't shy away from work. Work is your life blood. If you ever get depressed, just get back to work. You love a task that meets your drive.

♑

You use time well.

You have a great relationship with time. You are punctual and you use time well. You can achieve a great deal in a short amount of time. Time is your friend. You value time. And you value the time of others. You have an uncanny sense of the exact time at any given moment.

♑

You are steadfast.

You are unwavering. Once you've inwardly committed, there's no turning back. You keep your eye on the prize. You set your pace. You show up. You see it through. You are undeterred.

You apprentice to
the mountain of the spirit.

Sometimes we climb the mountain
of material accomplishment and
sometimes we climb the mountain
of our spiritual life. No matter
what your spiritual path IS, dear
Capricorn, you wish to delve ever
deeper. You are interested in
true initiations of consciousness!
You want to penetrate the
mysteries of life.

♑

You love order.

You might love a good five year plan. Or a clean, clear desk. You might like to plan the entire trip on a map before you take it. Or make reservations ahead of time for everything. You love knowing what's going to happen and then you love watching it unfold in just that way!

You abide by the Law.

Well, there are rule breakers and rule followers. You tend to follow the rules. You believe the Laws are there for a reason and you like to be a responsible citizen. Of course, you are just as willing and determined to address and take down Laws that are corrupt.

You lead.

You will willingly be at the front
of the line in even the most
difficult of circumstance. You
quietly and purposefully lead
the way. You don't want or need
a lot of attention. You ask simply
that people fulfill their assigned
work. You know how to get to the
mountain top and will lead the
way. You ask only for commitment
and seriousness of purpose.

♑

You are patient and pragmatic.

You know that everything takes time. You do not give up easily and will wait until the right moment to take the right step. You will not be rushed. And because you have an excellent sense of timing, you are willing to be patient and select the perfect moment to move forward.

♑

You are independent.

You generally go it alone, Capricorn. It's hard to climb side by side as you are scaling the mountain. You often feel that others don't have the same desire to succeed as you do. You set off solo and are often happiest when you are on your own.

You are good at setting boundaries.

You are clear about what is and is not acceptable. You have no issues with drawing a line in the sand. You know what you expect and if others don't show up with equal commitment, you happily dismiss, say 'No' or refuse entry.

♑

You are good with money.

You know how to make it, save
it, and grow it. You are careful.
You don't take huge risks when it
comes to your financial well-being.
You put time and energy into
making the money and you will
invest it wisely.

♑

You are serious about loving
whom you love.

You like to take care of loved
ones. You like to provide for
their needs and their wishes.
You often show your love in very
practical ways. You'll buy your
loved one new tires if that's
what they need.

Living Your Capricorn Love

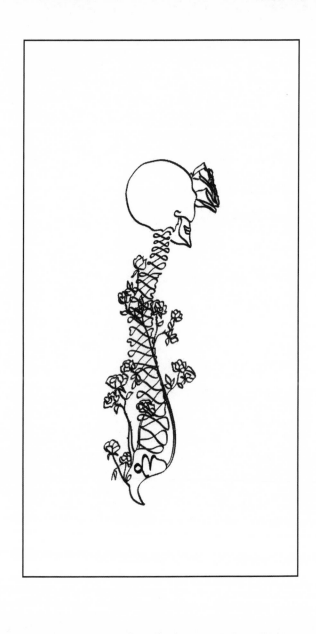

How are you feeling, dear Capricorn? Can you sense the potency of your gifts? Do you want to make the very most of this earthy energy of Capricorn? Here are some thoughts about how to live fully into your Capricorn love and how to nourish your Capricorn spirit. Consider them little whispered reminders meant to help you THRIVE. Consider them 'action items' — a loving Capricorn "to-do" list. Consider them invitations to live your fullest earthiest purpose.

Parent something or someone.

You already know how to take care of business and everyone in the room. Choose someone or something that is like your child. Be responsible to it. Encourage its growth. Shepherd it.

Make a 5 year plan.

My Great Uncle Leon always loved a good 5 year plan. It can change after all. But it's great to know where you are headed and how you're going to get there.

Breathe in your own authority.

No one else is going to do this for you. Breathe in your capability, maturity, commitment. Breathe in the fact that you know you can do this. Breathe in your excellence and your masterful ways. Now, walk through that door and lead the way.

Create healthy routines.

Make sure there's more to life than work. Move your body. Spend time with friends. Make more time for pleasure. Eat well. Rest. Don't live with the bare minimum of self-care. Be responsible to yourself as well.

Create a schedule.

You do love time after all. Use it well. Make room for a variety of endeavors. Work, play, rest. Build in periods of nothingness as well. Don't cram or drive yourself too hard. Build in rest stops on your climb.

♑

Take good care of
your teeth, your knees,
and your bones!

Capricorn rules the skeleton.
It rules all the hard parts of
your body. Don't let them get
fragile or rigid. Take care to
keep flexible. Always think about
working with greater ease and
more fluidity.

Growing Your Capricorn Love

Sometimes, dear Capricorn, we swing too far in one direction and need to invite a balancing energy to set us right. We are all growing and need to address the parts of ourselves that have not developed as fully. The opportunity for Capricorn is to invite Cancer (your opposite sign) into the picture. Here are ways to grow your Capricorn love to be more revealing, sensitive and inclusive."

Practice articulating what you feel.

You have the tendency to manage or control your feelings, dear Capricorn. Practice naming what you are feeling with those that you trust. It's not healthy to keep it all tucked away and managed perfectly. And when you are able to articulate what you feel, your friends and loved ones can actually help!

Lighten up.

Easier said than done. But now and then, have a good laugh at your own intensity. Life is not about deadlines. And financial success is far from the only measurement for a life well lived. And breaking a few of your own rules every now and then is good for the spirit.

Play.

I know. This isn't easy. There's so much work to do. But occasionally put the work down. You don't have to sing and dance — but a good game of Monopoly or Sorry or Operation now and then would be good for your spirit. Let your kid-self out to play. Or ask yourself, "What does my version of play look like?"

Be spontaneous.

Everything does not need to be planned, dear Capricorn. Shred the schedule now and then and say, 'Yes' to an impromptu date. It will feel like a relief to shake things up now and then. It's good to work the muscles of flexibility and spontaneity.

♑

Think less of status or position.

Yes! You want to excel and be the best at what you do. And you like to hang out with people that are the best at what THEY do. But try not to fixate on power or money or position. Don't dismiss those along the way who may not have the trappings of success. A title isn't everything. The summit is only a moment at the end of an extraordinary journey.

Practice receiving the care of another.

You are so used to taking care of everyone. See how it feels to let a loved one care for you. Receive nourishment. Receive fully. Don't try to fix, manage, or control this situation. Your role is to breathe in the love being offered. That's it.

Spend time at home.

You are so often out in the world
working. Let your home be a
source of comfort. Spend some
time in the kitchen. Make soup.
Curl up by a fire. Rest. Replenish
before your next climb.

♑

Work it out with Dad.

That is, work to resolve your
own inner father issues, dear
Capricorn. Feel into the ways you
are living your life that may be
in some ways tied to the father
relationship — for good or ill.
Breathe in your own parental
energy and refuse to carry the
old story.

♑

Go to You-tube and look up "Goats Singing."

It's actually more like "goats screaming" but it is hilarious. And there is no way you can keep a straight face watching and listening to these goats. And you are the mountain goat, after all. You may actually need to watch repeatedly.

♑

Loosen your Grip.

We can't control everything,
Capricorn. And it can be very
exhausting trying to do so.
Practice delegating. Practice
letting go. Practice releasing
the belief that if you're not
guiding the ship, it will surely sink.
Surrender and receive!

Questions to Inspire
Sharing Your Capricorn Love

Dear Capricorn, here are a few questions and prompts that might inspire or clarify your mission. Grab your journal. Write for 15 minutes about each. Address one every day for awhile. Read your answers out loud to a friend. Let this exploration spark your next purposeful action.

♑

Here is some of the work
I love to do...

♑

Today I will be
patient with...

♑

I bring my presence
and stillness to...

♑

If I could climb
one mountain, it would be
the mountain of...

♑

Here are some of the most
crazy, spontaneous things
I've done in my life...

♑

Mountains or ocean?
And why?

♑

I want to loosen up
in these ways...

♑

What am I meant to parent?

♑

What are three things I am feeling right now? What is the next layer under each of those three feelings?

One Last Little Love Note:

Capricorn, I hope those questions spark new depth, purpose, and play(!) in your life. You have so much to offer, so much to give. And your clarity and leadership inspire so many. If you ever need encouragement, just dip into this little book for a reminder of your light.

Now go forth Capricorn, and do your thing.

The World is Waiting for YOU.

Big love,
Heidi Rose

About the Author.

Heidi grew up with an astrologer father and an architect mother. Her father taught her the zodiac with her ABC's and her mother taught her to love art and appreciate the beauty of the natural world. She likes to call herself a poet with a map of the heavens in her pocket. Her passion is to inspire and encourage us all to be our truest, most authentic, radiant selves using the tools of astrology and poetry.

www.heidirose.com
Instagram @heidiroserobbins